Ideas That Changed the World

THE FOUR KEY GOSPEL TRUTHS AND PEOPLE OF THE REFORMATION

DOMINIC STEELE

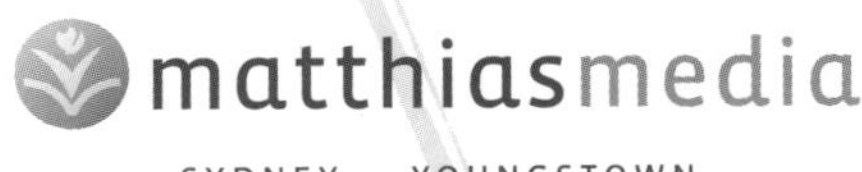

Ideas That Changed the World
Second edition
© Dominic Steele 2017

First edition 2007

Matthias Media
(St Matthias Press Ltd ACN 067 558 365)
Email: info@matthiasmedia.com.au
Internet: www.matthiasmedia.com.au
Please visit our website for current postal and telephone contact information.

Matthias Media (USA)
Email: sales@matthiasmedia.com
Internet: www.matthiasmedia.com
Please visit our website for current postal and telephone contact information.

ISBN 978 1 922206 20 6

Cover design and typesetting by Lankshear Design.

Contents

Introduction

When I was 19, I left the big smoke of Sydney and headed to the country to work as a radio station disc jockey at the only station in northern New South Wales that didn't play country music (2MO Gunnedah).

On my first Sunday in town I went along to St Joseph's Catholic Church. At that stage I think you could have counted on two hands the number of Sundays in my life that I hadn't been to mass.

On my second Sunday at mass I was invited to join the church council. I thought I was too young, but I was encouraged to stand and was appointed.

I had been christened and I participated in confession, communion and confirmation in the Roman Catholic Church. I had attended a Catholic school for eight years and served as an altar boy at mass for five years. Now I was on the church council.

However, in the months that followed I became increasingly disillusioned with Gunnedah's priest and church. It came to a head when in a homily during mass he criticized something I had said on the radio. I left that day (not the church of Rome, but the church in Gunnedah).

When I moved back to Sydney I went back to my family's parish church at Pennant Hills. I'd been there virtually every Sunday for 15 years (apart from the past 15 months). But no-one said, "Hello Dominic. We've missed you!"

I'd grown up belonging to the Catholic Church, but felt I didn't belong any more. Either I'd rejected church or church had rejected me. But I still knew that God existed and somehow things needed to be fixed with God.

When my friend Russell Powell invited me to his Protestant church and I eventually (and nervously) accepted his invitation, I was astonished at the differences.

There wasn't the same ceremony. But there was an authenticity that I hadn't seen before. Instead of walking straight out to the car park after receiving communion, people stayed for hours talking about the things they had been taught from the Bible.

Having been in church for years (and then out of church for a while), I would say (shockingly) that I became a Christian on 26 January 1986. That's when I began a personal relationship with God through Jesus.

After this I spent a long time working out how my new faith differed from the faith of my childhood.

Growing up, I wouldn't have said that I was saved by God's grace alone. I trusted in my own works to make me right with God rather than having faith alone in what Christ alone had done. And my authority came from the church institution rather than from the Bible alone.

I have come to see that these differences are enormously significant.

In this course we will travel together to Wittenberg, Geneva, London, Antwerp and Oxford to see the massive impact of the four key Reformation ideas: that we are saved by grace alone (by God's gracious initiative in Jesus); that salvation is made available to us through faith alone (not by us being good enough); that we know God through the Bible alone (and not through any church authority); and that we can pray to the Father through Christ alone (and not through the saints).

Dominic Steele

Idea 1: Faith alone

Martin Luther and faith alone

Martin Luther (1483-1546)

Martin Luther was born in Saxony, Germany, in 1483. He went to university in Erfurt, where he graduated with two degrees in 1505. Luther was set to study law, but a narrow brush with death by lightning is said to be the reason behind his decision to become an Augustine monk in 1506.

Luther was horrified at the corruption within the church of his day, and despaired at his own sinfulness. Still, he continued his theological study, taking on a third degree in 1512. But he was profoundly changed by reading Paul's letter to the Romans:

> For in [the gospel] God's righteousness is revealed from faith to faith, just as it is written: The righteous will live by faith. (Romans 1:17)

Luther realized that the righteousness of God was not primarily a *characteristic* of God to be feared, but an *activity* of God. God is righteous when he declares that the unrighteous who have faith shall be righteous.

Seeing that we are justified by faith and not by what we do meant that Luther could not sit by while poor peasants were offered salvation for their dead parents in exchange for money at a Roman Catholic fundraiser.

Luther drew up ninety-five theses for debate, which he posted upon the door of Wittenberg's Castle Church in 1517. He rejected the Catholic teaching that sin could be absolved through papal indulgences, since grace was given by God alone.

When Luther's theses were printed and distributed through Europe there was a huge backlash against the church. Papal indulgences dropped across the continent as people understood that they could be made right with God through faith in Christ's sacrifice rather than through human effort or giving money to the church.

In 1521 Luther was pressured to formally retract his teachings. Instead, in front of the Emperor, the princes and the papal hierarchy, Luther famously declared:

> If, then, I am not convinced by proof from Holy Scripture... and if my judgment is not in this way brought into subjection to God's word, I neither can nor will retract anything... I stand here and can say no more.[1]

Personally discovering faith alone

Christine Semple

Growing up in a Maltese Catholic family in Wagga Wagga, NSW, I think I always believed that God existed; yet Jesus had no real place in my life. God was someone who was real but too hard to understand. I used to think that if I was good enough then God should be happy with me. In order to please God, I used to do things like help people and give to charities.

The first time I was challenged to think seriously about what I believed was when I moved to Sydney and met some Protestant Christians. These people took the Bible seriously, and (astonishingly) wanted to live out what the Bible said.

They encouraged me to read the Bible, and I soon realized that the things I thought about God weren't right. I had trusted in being a good person as the right way to go, whereas the Bible said that it wasn't about my good works, but rather trusting that Jesus' death and resurrection were enough to save me. This was a challenge for me, as I had always believed in working for your reward.

As a Catholic, grace was a concept I didn't understand. But when I read the Bible I learned that grace is God's free gift of life — it is his way of saving us. Learning that salvation wasn't a result of anything I had done was a big change for me. Faith was also a strange concept to me as a Catholic. I thought of faith as a tangible thing — something that I needed to *do*. I thought that if I worked hard enough, then I would earn a faith I could lean on. But I read a passage in the Bible that said:

> For you are saved by grace through faith, and this is not from yourselves; it is God's gift — not from works, so that no one can boast. (Ephesians 2:8-9)

Reading this was amazing for someone like me, who had always thought that the

onus was on me to do enough good things to be right with God. This was a new concept that said there was nothing I could do; it was purely God's gift, and all I needed to do was trust in him.

Faith suddenly became about trusting what Jesus had done. I now understood that I could have a relationship with God personally through trusting in the person of Jesus. This changed faith from being something I needed to do to being a trust in God. I discovered that it wasn't all about what I was doing; it was all about Jesus.

Discussion 1: Faith alone

Watch: The medieval world, sin and salvation (7:30)

Discuss

The medieval Roman Church taught that everyone was sinful and owed a debt to God because of their disobedience—everyone from the highest king to the lowliest beggar. But what does God say?

Read Romans 3:9-20.
1. What does God say about the human condition? How does this make you feel?

2. Martin Luther said his first reading of this passage made him feel guilty and miserable. Do Luther's feelings resonate with you?

3. How do people seek to be justified (or declared righteous)?

4. Why do these attempts fail?

Watch: Martin Luther and justification by faith (4:40)

Discuss

It was while wrestling with the first chapter of Paul's letter to the Romans (especially Romans 1:16-17) that Martin Luther came to see that we are not saved by our own efforts.

Read Romans 1:16-17.
5. By whose power are people saved?

6. How are people saved?

Read Romans 3:21-26.
7. In the margin notes of his Bible, Luther wrote that Romans 3:21-26 was "the chief point, and the very central place of the Epistle, and of the whole Bible".[2] Why do you think Luther made this comment?

8. What does this passage say about faith and faith *alone* in regard to being justified (or declared righteous)?

9. How does Paul's teaching in Romans 3:21-26 contrast with the medieval
    Roman Catholic understanding of Luther's day?

Personal reflection
10. Romans 3 tells us that "all have sinned" (v. 23), but only "the one who has faith
    in Jesus" is declared righteous (or justified; v. 26). Where do you stand?

11. Have you put your faith in Jesus, as Martin Luther did?

Watch: Wittenberg to the world (6:15)

Discuss

Read Romans 5:1-5.
12. How does God declare you to be righteous (or justified) (v. 1)?

13. How do you obtain access to God's grace (vv. 1-2)?

Read Romans 5:6-9.
14. What did you do to deserve Christ's death for you (vv. 6, 8)?

15. What works did you or can you contribute to your salvation (v. 6)?

16. Considering Martin Luther's 'monstrous uncertainty'[3] about his standing before
    God, how do you think he would have felt after reading these verses? How do
    you feel?

Personal reflection
17. Do you have faith in what God has done in declaring you righteous through
    the death of Jesus?

18. Are you justified by faith in Jesus Christ alone?

Pray

NOTES

1   WJ Bryan (ed.), *The World's Famous Orations*, vol. VII, *Continental Europe (380-1906)*, Funk and
    Wagnalls, New York, 1906, p. 43.
2   Cited in DJ Moo, *The Epistle to the Romans*, NICNT, Eerdmans, Grand Rapids, 1996, p. 218.
3   In J Pelikan and HT Lehmann (eds), *Luther's Works*, vol. 26, *Lectures on Galatians, 1535, Chapters
    1-4*, ed. J Pelikan and WA Hansen, Concordia, Saint Louis, 1963, p. 386.

John Calvin and grace alone

John Calvin (1509-1564)

John Calvin is the second of our featured thinkers. Calvin is, after Augustine, the most influential theologian since the writing of the New Testament. He was born in 1509 in north-western France. By the time he went to the University of Paris, the Protestant Reformation was having a significant impact across Europe.

Calvin was forced to flee Paris in 1534 when, in a Roman Catholic crackdown, his mentor Nicolas Cop (the rector of the University of Paris) was accused of heresy over a lecture that it is thought Calvin helped him to write.

In 1536 Calvin stopped over in Geneva as he journeyed to Strasbourg. It was here that he was convinced by a fellow Reformer, William Farel, to stay and work to reform the church in Geneva. This became his major life's work.

Five hundred years after it was published in 1536, Calvin's *Institutes of Christian Religion* is still one of the most influential and significant theological works ever written. In the *Institutes* Calvin shows that it is by the grace of God alone that we can approach a holy God, through the redemptive work of Jesus Christ. He explains that it is not of ourselves that we can attain salvation by works of some kind, but that it is a gift from God alone. As Calvin wrote: "Faith, then, brings a man empty to God, that he may be filled with the blessings of Christ."[1]

Calvin had a very organized mind. He organized Protestant theology and the Geneva Church, taking the church away from the traditional Catholic order of worship. His reforms influenced the whole city as he attempted to bring everything — be it cultural, economic, social or political activity — under the lordship of Jesus Christ.

Under Calvin's lead, Geneva moved from being one of Europe's most immoral cities to being the Protestant capital of the Reformed Church.

Personally discovering grace alone

Jasper Lee

I was born in Australia into a first-generation migrant family from South-East Asia. When I was a young boy my family was part of a large Asian Catholic community of migrant families in Sydney. I was baptized into the Catholic Church and remember my first experiences of going to church. In the mid-80s, we moved church to our local parish in Marsfield.

My experience was mixed. I was profoundly unhappy at my Catholic school, and found church dry and ritualistic.

I knew who God was, but even at a young age I found him to be remote and unattainable. Like every 'good Catholic boy' I did the sacraments hoping that this would change my relationship with God, but somehow I didn't find the answers I was looking for.

In 1994 my parents switched to a Baptist church. They were dissatisfied with the traditional form of church and wanted my sister and me to meet more young people.

At this new church I was introduced to the Bible in a meaningful way. I was in a Bible study group with people my age, and for the first time I was introduced to the Jesus of the Bible. Until then, for me Jesus had been a good teacher and an example to follow, but I had not seen him as lord of my life and saviour of the whole world. Gradually, over a few years (influenced by some very patient youth group teachers), I became a Christian.

What had changed? Looking back I realize that growing up I did not have an understanding of God's grace. My religion revolved around obeying the commandments and *doing* things in order to attempt to be right with God. In many ways I understood the areas of my life where I wasn't perfect, and I struggled with guilt. I tried to deal with my sin by either trying to do better or simply downplaying what was wrong with my life.

Now I see that fundamentally, along with all humanity, I cannot meet the standards of a righteous and holy God. I need a saviour. God in his grace provided Jesus, who died on the cross so that I might have a relationship with him.

Discussion 2: Grace alone

Watch: John Calvin and grace (7:00)

Discuss

John Calvin said, "God declares, that he owes us nothing; so that salvation is not a reward or recompense, but unmixed grace".[2]

Read Ephesians 2:1-10.

1. How is the idea of grace being "unmixed", and "not a reward or recompense", spelled out in this passage?

2. What do the following verses tell us God does?
    - verse 5
    - verse 6
    - verse 8

3. Why does God do these things (vv. 4, 7)?

4. Where does faith come from (v. 8)?

John Calvin said, "If, on the part of God, it is grace alone, and if we bring nothing but faith, which strips us of all commendation, it follows that salvation does not come from us".

5. What good works do we contribute to our salvation (v. 9)?

Personal reflection

6. Do you really believe in the idea of 'grace alone'?

7. Has God made you alive?

Watch: The Libertines (7:25)

Discuss

Read Ephesians 2:10.
8.   What is God's purpose for those he has saved by grace?

9.   How did the Libertines get this wrong?

Read Titus 2:11-14.
10. What is God's aim in extending his grace to us (v. 14)?

11. How does grace teach us to live until Jesus returns (vv. 11-12)?

12. A Libertine might say, "Christians are free to sin because they're covered by the grace of God anyway". How do you think the apostle Paul or Calvin might have responded to that Libertine argument?

Watch: Grace today (3:55)

Discuss

Read Luke 18:9-14.
13. What does Jesus' story of the Pharisee and the tax collector illustrate about God's grace?

Pray

> **Sanctification**
> John Calvin says that a believer's union with Christ will lead to their sanctification—by which he means the process where an individual believer grows in holiness. Calvin taught that when God extends his grace to someone, and they receive Christ by faith, then they receive Christ's Spirit. For Calvin, the Holy Spirit is the agent through which saved people are made holy (or sanctified; 2 Thessalonians 2:13).

NOTES

1   J Calvin, *Commentaries on the Epistles of Paul to the Galatians and Ephesians*, trans. WM Pringle, Calvin Translation Society, Edinburgh, 1854, p. 227.
2   Calvin, p. 227.

William Tyndale and Bible alone

William Tyndale (1494-1536)

William Tyndale is one of the most significant figures in English history. He gave the nation its first English Bible and in doing so gave the country a unified language.

William Tyndale was born in England and studied theology at Oxford. At university he was horrified that there were no subjects on the Bible as part of his degree, so he formed small reading groups of fellow students to study the Bible in the evenings. Later he made it his life's work to produce a Bible for the common man. He said to a corrupt clergyman that if God spared his life, he would cause a boy that drives the plough to know more of the Scriptures than he did.[1]

The Catholic Church in England would not allow the production of the English Bible, so Tyndale worked in secret in Germany. In 1526 Tyndale completed translating the first English New Testament. Despite strenuous efforts by Catholic bishops and other church officials (including the burning of Bibles and people), thousands of copies of Tyndale's New Testament were printed and smuggled into England.

In 1535, while working on translating the Old Testament from Hebrew into English, Tyndale was arrested and imprisoned. After a year in jail he was sentenced to death by strangulation and burning. As Tyndale died, his final cry encapsulated his unwavering mission to bring the word of God to the people: "Lord! Open the king of England's eyes."[2]

Shortly after his death the political tide turned in England, and Tyndale's Bible was published legally under another name.

Personally discovering Bible alone

Mark Gilbert

I grew up going to Catholic schools, and had a generally positive experience in the Catholic Church. I didn't know many people outside the Catholic Church growing up, but this changed when I went to university. When I started university I became friends with many people who called themselves Christians.

The big question that got me was when these Christians asked me *why* I believed what I did. I hadn't really thought much about that. So I answered, "Because the priest says…" But I knew that wasn't a satisfying answer.

I was impressed that the people I met had reasons for why they believed what they believed, based on their knowledge of the Bible. They could say they knew God as he truly is due to what they read in the Bible. What they said was somewhat different to what I knew about God, so I wanted to know the Bible more — essentially so that I could correct them.

I was excited to read in the Bible about what God was like, and my understanding became a lot clearer. Over the next six months I became convinced of a key belief that I had not learnt in the Catholic Church. This was that I was right with God not on the basis of how good I was or anything I had done, but through faith alone in what Jesus Christ had done for me. There was nothing I could do to earn God's favour. This concept kept on coming up again and again over my six months of reading, and I came to trust in what the Bible says. It struck me that the Bible teaches something different from what I was taught in the Catholic Church.

I started to date a girl (who is now my wife), and once we started going out I was keen for us to go to the same church together. When I went to visit her church — my first time at a Protestant church — I was really impressed that the Bible was taught clearly and powerfully, and I was impressed that what people learned from the Bible actually changed their lives. People would hang around after church to discuss how God's word was changing their lives in terms of their careers and friends.

So I met with a friend from university who had left medicine to train to be a minister. We sat down with Vatican II documents and the book of Galatians. By looking at those two documents I became convinced that the Catholic Church wasn't merely misguided but was actually teaching a different message.

I realized that Roman Catholicism was putting the historical traditions of the church on the same level as the Bible. However, in my reading of the Bible I'd seen that traditions are not a substitute for the word of God. The Bible sits above any church traditions — and this is a very different message to what I had learned growing up.

Discussion 3: Bible alone

Watch: A Bible for the ploughboy (8:35)

Discuss

1. Why didn't the Roman Church want an accessible English translation of the Bible?

2. Read the following verses and note down what each verse tells us about the word of God, and what part God expects his word to play in the life of a Christian believer:
   - Acts 20:32
   - 1 Corinthians 10:11-12
   - Ephesians 6:17
   - Hebrews 4:12
   - 2 Peter 1:20-21

3. Why is access to the Bible in your own language important?

4. How does the word of God feature in your life?

Watch: Lord, open the King of England's eyes (7:30)

Discuss

Read 2 Timothy 3:14-17.
5. What does Paul say here about:
   - the authority of the Scriptures?
   - the purpose of the Scriptures?
   - the sufficiency of the Scriptures?

6. What questions should you ask as you read *any* text of Scripture?

Watch: A Bible in English (3:55)

Discuss

Read Psalm 19:7-11.

7. What are the characteristics of the word of the Lord?

8. What does following the word of the Lord lead to?

Personal reflection

9. Think back on Paul's challenge in 2 Timothy 3:14-17. How do we "continue in what [we] have learned and firmly believed"?

10. Have you been regularly reading and reflecting upon the word of God? What practical changes can you make to prioritize this?

Pray

NOTES

1   J Fox, *Fox's Book of Martyrs: The Acts and Monuments of the Church*, ed. J Cumming, vol. 2, George Virtue, London, 1844, p. 394.
2   Cited in Fox, p. 400.

Idea 4: Christ alone

Thomas Cranmer and Christ alone

Thomas Cranmer (1489-1556)

Thomas Cranmer was the most significant figure in the Protestant Reformation in England. He was Archbishop of Canterbury (i.e. leader) of the Church of England when the church broke away from Rome. Born in Nottinghamshire in 1489, Cranmer became Archbishop of Canterbury in 1533 under Henry VIII.

In 1548, with the support of Henry's son Edward VI, Cranmer replaced parts of the Latin Mass with English (prayer and confession). He put an English Bible in every parish church, and started reworking the Mass itself.

The following year Cranmer published a new English prayer book (which he improved in 1552), rejecting the central Catholic teaching of transubstantiation (i.e. that the bread and wine actually became the body and blood of Christ). Cranmer taught that Jesus Christ alone is the perfect sacrifice for our sins and therefore there is no need for a continued priestly sacrifice. Under Cranmer, Holy Communion stopped being a sacrifice and became a remembrance meal.

When Edward died and Catholic 'Bloody' Queen Mary took the throne, she executed almost 290 protestant dissenters, including Archbishop Cranmer.

In jail awaiting execution, Cranmer cracked and recanted of his Protestantism. However, in the moments before his execution, he switched again, recanting his previous recantation and reaffirming his rejection of Catholicism. As he was being burnt Cranmer forced his right arm — the arm that had scribed the original recantation — into the flames in a visual display of allegiance to the Bible's teaching of Christ's sacrifice once for all.

Personally discovering Christ alone

Elizabeth Clarke

I went to Catholic schools as a child, and felt very committed to my Catholic faith. I always attended church. I brought my children up going to church. I made a lot of effort to make sure they understood mass and prayed. I was very anxious that they hold onto the Catholic faith, and I was able to convince their father that they should go to a Catholic school.

Looking back, I took on board what suited me in the Catholic Church and rejected the rest (things like confession and rules about contraception). But as I got into my forties I started to think through what I believed, and it all seemed too vague.

I started to meet with a group of work colleagues to pray. They would bring along their Bibles, so I started to bring along my Bible. But then I realized I didn't really know how to read the Bible. So they introduced me to study guides, which I started to use to read the Bible. As I read the Bible it opened up my eyes to so many things I was being taught in the Catholic Church that were irrelevant to faith in Jesus Christ.

Then one of the women in the group I was praying with said, "This is amazing. Jesus died to save us from our sins. We are no longer seen as sinners before God." I had an incredible realization that this was true. Up until then I had the head knowledge, but not the heart knowledge. Then all of a sudden the superstition evaporated. And the burden of whether or not I would go to heaven if I dropped dead tomorrow disappeared. I suddenly had assurance of God's gift of salvation.

Initially I felt very angry with the Catholic Church about those years of being misled over how we can relate to God (through the saints and Mary) rather than through Christ alone. Now I just feel sad.

As my sister was dying of cancer, her Catholic in-laws in Ireland were holding masses and novenas for her. And they kept sending her relics. I was able to talk to her about how these things aren't necessary, and how you can speak directly to God in prayer through Christ alone. She accepted the gifts of relics, but I don't think she ever thought they were going to help her to be healed, or that she needed them to assist in her prayers.

I remember my brother asking me how to pray the Rosary (a Roman Catholic prayer that involves repeating 50 times the prayer "Hail Mary"). I pointed him to Psalm 23 and Psalm 139 and encouraged him to pray the Lord's Prayer. As far as I know that's what he did.

I now constantly pray for revival in the Catholic Church, from the top to the bottom, that they might teach that we can be saved through Christ alone.

Discussion 4: Christ alone

Watch: The Reformation in England (5:15)

Discuss

Thomas Cranmer moved the English church away from the medieval misunderstanding of sacrifice.

Read Hebrews 9:1-10.
1.   List the activities involved in Old Testament sacrifice.

2.   What were the difficulties with that sacrificial system? (See especially verses 8-10.)

Read Hebrews 9:11-22.
3.   What is the significance of blood in this passage? (See especially verse 22.)

4.   What has the blood of the Christ achieved? (See especially verses 12-14.)

Read Hebrews 9:23-28.
5.   Why has Jesus' sacrifice superseded the old system of sacrifice?

6.   Does the writer see the sacrifice of Christ as something repeated/repeatable, or as something that happened just once?

Watch: A crude and monstrous fiction (6:55)

Discuss

Read 1 Corinthians 11:23-34.
7.   What is the purpose of the Lord's Supper?

8.   As we celebrate the Lord's Supper, should we think of it as a sacrifice or as a remembrance?

9.   How should we go about celebrating the Lord's Supper (vv. 27-29, 31, 33-34)?

Read 1 Timothy 2:1-6 (especially verses 5-6).

10. How is it possible for someone to approach God with "petitions, prayers, intercessions, and thanksgivings"?

11. What do these verses suggest about the Roman Catholic practice of praying to the saints and to Mary, asking them to mediate between God and us—as with the famous Roman Catholic prayer 'Hail Mary' (below)?

> Hail Mary, full of grace,
> the Lord is with thee.
> Blessed art thou among women,
> and blessed is the fruit of thy womb, Jesus.
> Holy Mary, Mother of God,
> pray for us sinners now
> and at the hour of our death.
>
> Amen.

Watch: Bishops burned for their faith (8:30)

Discuss

Read Hebrews 4:14-16.

12. How does Jesus' role as a great high priest affect our:
    - times of personal weakness?
    - assurance of salvation?
    - approach to God in prayer?

13. Have you drawn near to Jesus' throne to find mercy and grace?

Pray

A final note

These four key ideas — faith alone, grace alone, Bible alone and Christ alone — changed the world and profoundly affected the lives of the four key Reformers at the centre of the Reformation. For each of them, the process of reading the Bible, discovering God's grace through Christ alone, and putting their faith in Christ was the most important thing in their life. That has also been true for me, and I hope it's true for you.

It may be that in doing this course, God has personally revealed his grace to you. If that's the case, that's fantastic! If you are looking for some short Bible studies to get you started in reading the Bible, I recommend Matthias Media's *Tough Questions* and *Just for Starters*.

Or perhaps this course has helped you to better grasp the significance of what it means to be saved through the gospel of God's grace alone, through faith in Christ alone, having learned this faith through the Bible alone. If that's the case, let me encourage you to do this course again with a Roman Catholic friend, so that they might also better understand these ideas that changed the world and develop a personal relationship with Jesus.

If you would like to read further about the ideas that changed the world, you'll find some helpful resources below.

Other recommended and related books from Matthias Media

Stepping Out in Faith
Eleven true stories from very different people who have all been transformed by reading God's word for themselves.

Nothing in my Hand I Bring
Ray Galea shares his story of moving from a Roman Catholic to a Protestant faith, and in so doing he explains the important differences between them.

Right Side Up: Life as God meant it to be
A stirring book for new and established Christians about what it means (and what it's like) to live the Christian life… to live 'right side up'.

Faith: It's always been a matter of trust
A short book exploring what exactly faith is, why it's so important, what we're meant to have faith in, and what difference it should make to our everyday lives.

Hope: The best is yet to come
A short book that unpacks what the Bible has to say about hope — what it is (and isn't), and how it comforts, challenges and directs us as Christians.

Matthias Media is an evangelical publishing ministry that seeks to persuade all Christians of the truth of God's purposes in Jesus Christ as revealed in the Bible, and equip them with high-quality resources, so that by the work of the Holy Spirit they will:

- abandon their lives to the honour and service of Christ in daily holiness and decision-making
- pray constantly in Christ's name for the fruitfulness and growth of his gospel
- speak the Bible's life-changing word whenever and however they can—in the home, in the world and in the fellowship of his people.

Our resources range from Bible studies and books through to training courses, audio sermons and children's Sunday School material. To find out more, and to access samples and free downloads, visit our website:

www.matthiasmedia.com

How to buy our resources

1. Direct from us over the internet:
   – in the US: www.matthiasmedia.com
   – in Australia: www.matthiasmedia.com.au

2. Direct from us by phone: please visit our website for current phone contact information.

3. Through a range of outlets in various parts of the world. Visit **www.matthiasmedia.com/contact** for details about recommended retailers in your part of the world.

4. Trade enquiries can be addressed to:
   – in the US and Canada: sales@matthiasmedia.com
   – in Australia and the rest of the world: sales@matthiasmedia.com.au